The Feathered Heart

by Mark Turcotte

MARCH/Abrazo Press
Chicago

Acknowledgments

These poems first appeared in the following publications:
"Horse and Cradle," *Hammers*; "Indian Boys" and "Rain
Rain," *Hyphen Magazine*; "Sky Breathes Sky" and "Wedding,"
The Eagle; "Ten Thousand Thousand Bones," *Dark Night Field
Notes*.

Love and grace to my family, the old and new tribe.

Thanks to Vernon Blackdog Lee, Marc K. Smith, Michael
Warr and The Guild Complex, Word Ban'd, all the Dark
Night Relatives (Free Leonard Peltier), S.K. Power, Quraysh
Ali, Shana Mandel, Yorke Corbin, R. Russell and Carlos
Cumpián.

More love and grace to Bobbie Pankratz, Suzanne Frank,
Loyal Suntken and Jim Mottonen for the many years of
friendship and patience.

Cover art: *Two Worlds Hand*, by the author.
Illustrations: Kathleen S. Presnell.
Book design: Cynthia Gallaher.

Printed in the United States of America.
ISBN 1-877636-12-6 (paper).
Library of Congress Catalog Card Number 95-07540.

This project is partially supported by a Community Arts
Assistance Program Grant from the City of Chicago Depart-
ment of Cultural Affairs and Illinois Arts Council Access
Program.

The Feathered Heart
is dedicated to

my mother,
Dorothea Marie

Patti Smith and PSG,
whose words and music
saved my life
and showed me
the sea of possibilities

and

my wife, Kathleen,
who has given
all.

"I love to go wandering
out among the trees,
to listen to them whisper
as the wind blows through their leaves."
D.M. Demery

Contents

The Eye Shakes

I'm trying to remember what i do not remember. images
come in stuttering phrases, staccato, bent and broken,
as if seen through the spokes of a madly spinning wheel.
flickering black and white clattering into color. the eye
begins to shake, not wanting to remember.

images...images...images...

the rusted bed of a speeding pick-up truck. two children
hunkered down, hiding. a boy and a girl. gravel spattering
the underside of the truck. the boy lifts his head, peers
over the tailgate. a car is following, one headlight shining.
the boy sees, faintly, crouching upon the hood of the car,
the Devil laughing. the eye begins to shake...

Horse and Cradle

for Dorothea Marie

she white woman fell
in love with the
black wave
of his hair with
the way his
voice rose up out
of him from the earth the way
his flirtatious hands
fell over
the strings of his guitar

she fell white woman
in love with
the points
of his eyes the soft
circles they cut
through her shoulders
the way he
came to her bed dressed
in savage feathers
her bed
where she climbed upon his
copperbrown
horse of a back
where she
carried the arrow in
her heart she
became my mother
the gently ever gently
rocking cradle

of my soul.

Tiny Warriors

"Whose voice was first sounded on this land?"
Mahpiya Luta (Red Cloud)

Jesse and me we little boys
prance the top of the hill
galloping
our wind horses
through tall grasses whispering
low across our
brown backs

the voice of centuries
murmuring old tongues
forgotten in our ears
familiar
to the feather in our heart
remembered
in the frenzy of our blood

the voice of centuries
spinning sacred sunlight song
upon our heads
beneath our heels
we laughing, leaping
tiny warriors
ride and fall and ride and fall
we ride
and all fall down the hill

the whispers fading

the skin of our chests
stretched tight
over heaving *Ojibway* drums.

Ojibway: a Great Lakes and northern plains people.

Flies Buzzing

"somewhere in america, in a certain state of grace..."
Patti Smith

as a child i danced
to the heartful savage
rhythm
of the native the
american indian
in the turtle mountains
in the round hall
in the greasy light
of kerosene lamps

as a child i danced
among the long jangle legs
of the men down
beside the whispering moccasin women
in close circles
around the old ones
who sat at the drum
their heads tossed backs arched
in ancient prayer

as a child i
danced away from the fist
i danced toward the rhythm of life
i danced into dream into
    the sound of flies buzzing,
a deer advancing but clinging to the forest wall
the old red woman rocking in her tattered shawl
the women bent breasts drooping
to the mouths of their young
the heat hanging heavy on the tips of our tongues

until the sun
burned the sky black the moon
made us all silvery blue
and the night sounds the night sounds

folded together with the buzzing
still in our heads
becoming a chant of ghosts
of *Crazy Horse* and *Wovoka*
and all the endless others
snaking through the weaving through the
trees like
beams of ribbons of light
singing, *we shall live again we shall live,*

until the sun and the sun and the sun and i
awaken
still a child
still dancing.

Crazy Horse (c.1841-1877): Oglala Lakota warrior and dreamer.
Wovoka (c.1858-1932): Paiute spiritualist who resurrected the Ghost
Dance.

True Sign

he was
the first of all of them
in his sunday school class
to memorize the lord's prayer and
the first to mumble,
go to hell,
as he slumped in a pew
beside his mother

he knew it wasn't right
all of this
combing his hair tucking
in his shirt tail
saving his dimes
for the collection plate
getting down
on his knees
to pray

so he
would lie on his back
in the summer grass
of late sunday morning
and he would
watch the sky
for a true sign
from god

a hawk
arching toward the sun
loosing a feather
floating falling
to land upon his bare brown chest like
a true sign.

Indian Boys

one little
two little
three little
four little
five little
six little
seven little
eight little
nine little
ten little

under the moon
that perfect ruby sky fruit
indian boys pace
or carve through the nightness
in rusted cars
their thick lips
wetted glistening
with the breath of sick roses
and bad wine

while one sad feather swings
upside down
from the rearview mirror
brushing
catholic dust from
the head of a cracked
and yellow
dashboard madonna.

Room Still Full of Death

a flame
within a lamp
upon a table
against the wall
below a clock
dripping time
onto the floor
where shadows shake
the smell of earth
from the man's boots
as he listens
to the moan
of longing
from the corner
that is dark

and he whispers harshly,

sleep child
your mother
is lying deep.

Father's Dust

the child was struck
at a tender age
with
the dry mouth taste
of his father's dust

dust of lies
dust of rage
dust of wandering
dust of going going away

then finally
the dust of never returning

the child was struck
gasping for air
parched
left choking
on the memory
growing in his throat

for his father
made the earth shudder
beneath the fall
of his foot
for his father
made men tremble
beneath the gust
of his voice

for his father
ate the sky
with his teeth
and
with his hands

dragged deep scars
into the flesh
of hearts
of backs
of minds
into the flesh
of dreams

for his father
was the first
to bruise the child
with the fist of impatience
for his father
was the first
to rape the child
with the body of shame
for his father
was the first
to sting the child
with the tongue of hate

the child was struck
at a tender age
with
the dry mouth taste
of his father's dust

for his father
was the first
to make the child
want to spit.

Window Glass

he often found himself
late at night
looking
to the skies
    imagining the stars
as razors
scraping up against the
blackness as if
it were all just a painted over
    window glass and
somewhere beyond there was another light.

Sky Breathes Sky

earth woman i
am made
of you
the strong clay
of you
builds my bones
the soft clay

the milk
of you
falls in light
from my eyes

earth woman
your river rushes blood
in my hands rushes
in my hips
filling me

your sky breathes sky breathes
of me
your fire
lives on my voice
whispers

earth woman
the wind
of you
sighs rises
in my soul

the skin
of you
feathers my heart the bird
in my chest

that sings
at the scent sight
of you

earth woman i
am blessed
made
of you.

Flying With The Wind

he is gone into the dust
flying with the wind
over the turtle-backed hills
into the far and the far and the far

he is gone
into the trees
into the black earth
into the thick grass
beneath my belly
where i am
stretched out
cradling the pipe
and remembering him

his gnarled beadworking fingers
are gone
his squinting gaze
gone
his crooked mouth
his brittle bones
and their creaking
whenever he walked
whenever he reached
to scratch his scalp
with a stiff stubborn thumb

flying with the wind
his trembling voice
is gone
his clicking Cree tongue
his laughter
gone
with his wise heart
and its ever expanding embrace

and i roll over i stand
to the rising sun
i light the pipe and i lift it
to the highest point
    of the empty yellow sky

flying with the wind
he is gone
but for one puff
of smoke from somewhere.

Horse Dance

we dream
the pony of Crazy Horse
twisting
in a field
of yellow hair
its nervous neck
painted with
a hail of stones
stomp
step step
stomp
step step

we dream
the pony of Crazy Horse
dancing
in a field
of greasy grass
polishing its anxious hooves
upon the buttons
of Custer's coat
stomp
step step
stomp

we dream
the pony of Crazy Horse
leaping
in a field
of horses grazing
riderless
deaf to the distant wail of a widow
crying,
why my Georgie why my Georgie why,
stomp

we dream
the pony of Crazy Horse
rising
in a field
of bloodied flowers
where the horn
of her husband's empty saddle
is still decorated
with the flesh of Lakota women,
that is *why my Georgie why,*
stomp
step step
step step...

Recognize Stepfather

years later
after we
escaped you
and the reservation
i was seventeen strong
and still
very angry
and i was visiting there
when i recognized
you

i recognized you immediately
stumbling
from another barroom door
i recognized you immediately
leaning upon the wall
swaying toward me
and i recognized immediately
that i
was going to kill you

because i remembered it all
i remembered all of it

the little boy
standing on
the strawfilled
mattress screaming with
each click
of your fist
upon his mother's jaw

the little boy
with your boot bottomed
against his neck
smashing his face

into the dirt floor
the little boy
trying really trying
not to
let you
see him cry

the little boy
covering his head trying
not to listen to
the, *no no no daddy*,
of his big sister

the little boy
begging god just
to take
you away
then promising to do it
himself someday

because i remembered it all
i remembered all of it

and i recognized you
as you slipped
as my heart blackened
and i recognized you
as you fell
as my hands balled into fists
and i recognized myself
rushing upon you
yanking you up
by the collar baring my teeth
ready to break you in half
when i recognized
that you were too limp
that you were too weak
that you were too broken
to break

so i carried you across the street
into the warmth
of a late night laundry
propped you up
in a chair
daubed your spitty mouth
with my sleeve
and i
went back outside
and i

tried i really tried
not to cry.

Under Grey Gods

"I have seen for some time now the change in everything."
                                        Rilke

fall into autumn
where the hours lay cold
in the thin branches
and the leaves all scatter
erasing the ground
to pillow
against the fences lining
the field

i rest in the earth
in the furrows the folds
while
the plowers circle
and smoke the sky

here time is my breathing my breath
is slow
and i'm praying
to vanish
into grey gods dancing
in front of my eyes.

Folded Down

i remember it was
winter and
my hair was
longer than it had ever been

we were together in the basement
with that sweet smoky juice
invading our veins
and i remember
the ember reflecting in
her eye

some sound some sound was
waving at me
from two dark corners
when i reached
to open her she
just folded around my fingers
folded down
to the floor
as the ember dimmed away

i remember it was
and my hair was
and i leaned back into the wall
took a ride
on the elastic train of thought
it lasted all night and then some.

Indio

i was *el Indio*
the night of the dance
down along the border
whirling
i watched you whirl
to tejano guitars
while golden beckoning birds
flew from beneath
your shimmering skirt

my tequila fingers
reaching for you
trapped a bird
within your hem
and ripped the glimmering thread

you looked at me
as though
i had torn the moonlight
in half.

Leads You To Water

woman, i'm dreaming of you
    out there
on the desert
    out there
at the edge of the world
with your bare feet
padding down the dust
your eyes grazing
the red yellow
horizon

i send to you
the compass coyote
who wanders beside you
leads you to water leads you to water

where i'm waiting for you
to drink from my hands
like i was like i
was the land
and you
the thirsty sky.

The Boy Dances

The boy dances around the drum, his feet rise and fall.
sweat flies from his hair and sizzles in the circle. his
heart is a fist of blood clenched in the rhythm of the drum.
the boy dances, his feet rise and fall. he sees the woman
standing on the edge of the circle. the stark whiteness of
her hands, the whiteness of her face. her eyes, the light
in her eyes. the boy dances, his feet rise and fall. his
heart is a screaming wind, a hammer. demons fly from
his hair and flare in the circle. his feet rise and fall. her
eyes her eyes. the boy dances into the light...

Angels We

it is time for the choking dust
of the old and wispy one
to be brushed away
by the wings of
new angels we

it is time to let our shoulders rise
it is time to let our shoulders lift
it is time to let our shoulders open
into wings of glorious flame glorious
it is time to leap
into this coming night of chaos
once and finally
upon wings made of pure sun
it is time for victory
it is time for victory we.

Hands

old man
i stood over you
in your box
and when i reached
to touch your
grey folded hands

i remembered
a summer day
beside big water
when you laughed
and lifted me
higher than the trees

and i felt
like a big boy
like a big boy
in your hands
i felt
like a good boy
and you said, *hey do you*
  see any angels up there

old man
i leaned over you
in your box
touched my hands
into your
grey wave of hair
whispered,
may Grandfather give you feathers,
all is forgiven
down here.

This Wind

the stars
that fell last night hissing
in the wet street
they go on burning
guiding light
in this wind this you
that lives now forever in my hair
forever now at the tips of my fingers

this wind that walks
over my mouth some spider
dancing my lips
into a silken smile

this wind this you
that shapes
the mountain of my face
smoothing
away the old jagged peaks

this wind this you
that laces through the
lifts
the curtains in my heart one
by one

this wind this you
that sees me seizes me
carries me
warm and wildly human
through these chicago streets

this wind this you.

The Flower On

if you were
the flower on
    this blanket
resting soft upon my
  shoulder

i would whisper
  to you
my mouth against
    your petals
of the wings
that flutter over us
  while we sleep.

Feather

for Kathleen

long before this light
before that first
star was ever wished
    upon
you were a twinkle
in the universe's eye

you were the glint
    at the tip
of a feather
on the wing
of an angel you

are the one
that the old ones
came to know
that the old ones
    moaned of
scratched on walls about and

now and here
my hands my fingers dream
    of you
beyond touching and

now and here
when i press my head
to this pillow
your whispers rise flutter
through my hair your sighs
    shake
from these sheets wash
over my belly over my

hands somehow they
remember you
    feather
soft alive electric
somehow my shoulder
remembers
your sleeping face and
    darling
i have sweet dreams.

Wedding

our god has slept
and dreamed us here
and from the sweat of dream
comes the sweet scent
    of vision

we two within a northern wood
beside a lake of morning gold
we two before Grandfather's plume
nestled to the breast of our new tribe

here upon the earth
of my mothers
 i give you my eyes to see
 i give you my hand to lead
 i give you my breath to breathe
here beneath the sky
of my fathers
 i give you my soul to seek
 i give you my spirit to heal
 i give you my heart to hold

together we shall be this vision
 this water this wood
 this earth and sky
together we shall be this vision
 this birth this life this
      eternity.

Amber On Opal

nights
in the heated den
of our bed
two animals in
each others fur
nips and growls and groans
my thundering blood
drawn by your anxious claw

they become mornings
in the cool sheets
of our bed
man and woman
skin to skin
amber on opal
nips and growls and grins
my happy light
drawn by your laughing flower

together we make
scent
milk of dandelion.

Rain Rain

for Ezra Cole

hot flashes burn
tiny holes in my one
long cool memory

dreams scenes tumble
from my hair
into the rain slick street
flowing streams into
the gutter
oily rainbows
painting the feet of
ecstatic children dancing
in the puddles singing,
rain rain never go away,

and one small boy bends
blows bubbles in a pool
with a straw
he laughs splashes
down the street
glancing back at me
dreams scenes tumbling
from his
hair in strings
over his face.

Chippewa Hitch Hike

hitch-hiking last night (and
  in between
the shine
    of headlights) i fell

in love with

  the moon

again.

Motherdrum

motherdrum motherdrum

more than hushed
the rhythm crushed
muffled
beneath the weight
of plodding footsteps
turning wheels
and
smoking stacks

motherdrum motherdrum

sirens kill the night
the city
claws the stars
out of the sky
radios
do not wave they
eat the air and
tear the skin
from the trees

motherdrum motherdrum

sirens kill the night
the city
rapes my children
they gang
together
in the toxic alleys
they drown in neon
they drown in flashing signs
seek silence
in each other's blood

motherdrum motherdrum

sirens kill the night
the city
chases away
spirits from my hair
dreams from my reach
hope from my eyes

sirens kill the night
and i cannot hear

motherdrum motherdrum.

Ten Thousand Thousand Bones

for Joe Schranz

from long away from
behind museum doors from
darkly dusty rooms

i hear Grandmother
rattling she rattles
among ten thousand thousand bones
i hear Grandmother
rattling she rattles

she is frightened alone
among ten thousand thousand bones
taken from warm belly earth
hot heart of earth
that was her resting home

crying cold
shaking on the shelf alone
rattling
among ten thousand thousand bones.

•

we wait for you Grandmother
here in the wood
where you belong

the deer are stamping circles
scratching at the ground
leaning their ears
to listen for your song
but you are gone

the branches of the trees
all ache for you
with their roots below
that once cradled you
bending reaching
to hear your song
but you are gone

the river moans
your missing voice
the grass and stone
are silent
as they mourn
and listen listen

the wings of hawks
call out your name
and wonder wonder
where you've gone

answered only by your rattling
from where you shiver
cold alone
among ten thousand thousand bones

•

Grandmother do not forgive
them they know
what they have done

taken you from
sacred circle light
and left you
in their tomb
among all those other bones

fools
they refuse to hear
the anguish in the earth
the cry of fox and pheasant
in your home

fools
they refuse to fear
the angry step of spirit horse
whose hoof
shall make a rattling
in their own living bones

.

we wait for you Grandmother
here in the wood
where it's been so long

the deer are scratching circles
stamping at the ground
leaning their ears
to listen for your song

the branches of the trees
all ache for you
with their roots below
that once cradled you
reaching bending
to hear your song

the river moans
your missing voice
the grass and stone
are silent
as they mourn
and listen listen

the wings of hawks
call out your name
and wonder wonder
where you've gone

answered only by your rattling
from where you shiver
cold alone
among ten thousand thousand bones

Grandmother do not forgive
them they know
what they have done.

Dedicated to an ancient woman taken from the Earth near New Lenox, Illinois in the winter of 1993/94...and to the men and women who have stood in her honor.

Brother River Dreams

"I'm not Tonto..."
        E. Donald Two-Rivers

in ripples
becoming waves
unyielding he
unchanging he
flows down

from the woodlands
and the marshes
of northwest ontario
brother river dreams
and knifes his hungry way
into the fat and fleshy heart
of the places
where america is sleeping

brother river dreams
and glides the barren highway
city to city
and with his silvery untamed teeth he
rips into the infested skins
of the factories and the machine shops
with his untamed teeth
into the blistered skins
of the jails and the bars
his untamed teeth
into the rotting skins
of the school yards
the places
where america is sleeping

brother river dreams
and washes down
the canyons of chicago

splashing through the alleys
with the laughter of his rice gathering people
flooding the unforgiven streets
with the blood and cries of *Anishinaabe* ghosts
all drowning drowning drowning
the places
where america is sleeping

brother river dreams
he speaks the fire within our veins
he dreams he walks so we remain
and his blood never forgets your shame
so sleep on
america
we wake
and we are rising
while our brother river dreams.

Anishinaabe: Ojibway/Chippewa name for themselves, meaning
"the first people".

Last Drink

he thinks he
slouches at the bar
staring down
at the last drink
in the bottom
of his glass

he leans closer
the dark whiskey
begins to tremble
under the
weight of his breath
as his mind
rides the tiny ripples

he once lived
he thinks
in a house
made of logs
and mud and straw
woke in the mornings
to the sound of
dew slipping
along a blade of grass

lived on the side
of a hill
picked juneberries
as the soft brush
of Ojibway tongues
painted the sky
he thinks

remembers
the dusty grins
of sunbrown boys
chasing away the day
on tireless
stick ponies

his grandfather's hands
rough and careful
taking the skin
from a rabbit the silvery
muscle steaming
beneath
his hungry chuckle

he thinks
the women cooing
over baskets
over beadwork
over babies
the music of them
rising higher
than the mission bells

the summer
of the Potawatomi girl
who smelled of warm bread
fresh buttered
under his groping mouth
he remembers
he once lived

now wakes
on the street
with a chill
and the sun in his eyes
he thinks.

Half Blood

when my brother
loves me

he calls me
Anishinaabe

but when he does not
love me

he mentions
the paleness
of
my hands.

Song for the Endless Others

mornings at my kitchen table
drinking coffee
while the city rumbles low
i see the endless others
who live within the walls
as they linger
in the doorways
sit upon the window sills
spin blade to blade
fan to fan across the ceiling
and flutter to the floor

where my woman curls up tight
upon the bed
against her breast our drowsy son
i see the endless others
who between the blankets run
as they wrap
and as they weave
these two sleepers that i love
within soft dreams
that spread to wings and into wings
sweeping out across the floor

nights when i move about the city
smoking Luckys
shaking off the autumn chill
i see the endless others
sparking blue beneath the El
as they laugh
and as they dance
across the station walls
train to train
out into the streets to tangle
up the taxis in their hair

the endless others
watch my nights
give straightness
to my crooked hands
give me voice and give me voice
chant and chant
within my bones

the endless others
guide my days
medicine the scars
that fill my throat
give me voice and give me voice
chant and chant
within my feathered heart.

Growler

once tried to kill it

the dark animal
pacing in my chest
with all my demons
wrapped
around its tail

i built a fire
in the backyard
burned 18 years
of words
watched notebooks
curl into ash
and imagined
the spiral bones

the growler
writhing inside
ripped me open

pushed out a hesitant claw
and began to sing.

Winter

in dreamtime
it's winter
and
i lean back into a tree

my hair is long
silver with dusk
and my hands curl closed

  a little wind
stirs at my shoulder
the juice of darkness
crashes cold against my teeth

and then
the night is gone
and there
  is never another night.

Foreign Shore

"...the message is coated with static
steel clutter poking into the sky
the landscape eclipsed
by the shadows of devastation..."
                          Mick Vranich

the sky is
black and milky
as i rest
on this foreign shore
  feeling
like i'm looking down
from someplace
higher

all along the beach
the gulls sound
  together
lifting toward the stars
one giant wing

this would be
the perfect night
the perfect moment
for you to signal me
with your
alien frequency

there is no static now.

About the author...

Born of an Ojibway father and Irish-American mother, Mark Turcotte spent his earliest years on North Dakota's Turtle Mountain Reservation and in the migrant camps of the western United States. Later, he grew up in and around Lansing, Michigan. Winner of the first "Gwendolyn Brooks Open-Mic Poetry Award" (1993), he has also just completed a collection of poetry, *Songs of Our Ancestors*, for Childrens Press. He lives in Chicago with his wife, Kathleen, and their son, Ezra.

About MARCH/Abrazo Press

MARCH/Abrazo Press is the publishing arm of
Movimiento Artístico Chicano (MARCH, Inc.), which
was incorporated in Illinois in 1975 as a not-for-profit
cultural/arts organization. MARCH/Abrazo Press
publishes perfectbound books and chapbooks by and
about Native Americans, Chicanos and Latinos.

To order additional copies of this book, other MARCH/
Abrazo Press titles, or to be put on the mailing list,
write or call MARCH/Abrazo Press, P.O. Box 2890,
Chicago, Illinois 60690.

To arrange for presentations by Mark Turcotte or
other exciting MARCH/Abrazo poets and authors, call
(312)539-9638.